Everything You Need to Know About

# PLACING YOUR BABY FOR ADOPTION

Adoption is not about giving away your baby, adoption is about making a plan for your baby's life.

• THE NEED TO KNOW LIBRARY •

Everything You Need to Know About

# PLACING YOUR BABY FOR ADOPTION

Aliza Sherman

THE ROSEN PUBLISHING GROUP, INC.
NEW YORK

This book is dedicated to
Sara

Special thanks to K.K., Mary, Jane, Jen, and Leah.

Published in 1997 by The Rosen Publishing Group, Inc.
29 East 21st Street, New York, NY 10010

Copyright 1997 by The Rosen Publishing Group, Inc.

First Edition

Manufactured in the United States of America

**Library of Congress Cataloging-in-Publication Data**

Sherman, Aliza.
    Everything you need to know about placing your baby for adoption/
Aliza Sherman. — 1st ed.
      p.  cm. — (The need to know library)
    Includes bibliographical references and index.
    Summary: Provides teenage expectant parents the information needed
to make an informed decision regarding placing their baby for adoption.
    ISBN 0-8239-2266-9
    1. Adoption—United States—Juvenile literature.  2. Birthparents—
United States—Juvenile literature.  3. Teenage parents—United States—
Juvenile literature.  [1. Adoption.  2. Birthparents.  3. Teenage
parents.]  I. Title.  II. Title: Placing your baby for adoption.  III. Series.
HV875.55.S54  1997
362.7'34—DC20                        95-22427
                                                    CIP
                                                      AC

# Contents

# Introduction

If you are pregnant and thinking about adoption, you should understand exactly what the process involves. The more you know about the adoption process, the more easily you can decide whether adoption is the right choice for you.

This book will tell you what you need to know about adoption before you make any important decisions. It will discuss many of the emotional and legal issues involved in placing your baby for adoption.

If you decide on adoption, you will learn how to determine what type of adoption is right for you. Most importantly, you will learn about adoption resources and organizations to help you through the process.

In this book we do not say *keep* when referring to the decision not to place your baby. Instead, we say *parent*. The word "parenting" conveys all the hard work that raising a child requires. Many people use the term "giving up," or "surrendering" in discussing adoption. We use the term "place."

Learning that you are pregnant can be scary. But knowing all of
your options will help you feel more in control.

This term signifies the decision—your decision—
to choose a life for your baby.

Also, we usually refer to the baby as "your baby"
until the time of placement. The baby is legally
yours to parent until you sign the consent papers
waiving that right. Be aware of the way that the
agency, lawyer, or adoptive parents talk about your
baby when you are considering placement. Many
people feel that it will be easier for you to stop
thinking of the baby as yours. But it is okay for
you to say, "This is my baby. I want to make a
decision about my baby."

We will discuss many of the feelings you will
experience if you decide to place your baby, such
as sadness, loss, and anger. These feelings are
normal and natural. Many birth parents experience them. We will provide you with different
ways to help you cope with your feelings. There
are also stories from people who have felt many of
the same things that you do.

If you decide to place your baby, you might
need to find an agency to help you through the
process. Or you might need to find a lawyer. We
will discuss what to look for in each. The help list
in the back of the book offers information on
organizations that provide support, knowledgable
information, and counseling.

Be aware that as birth parents, you can decide
to place your baby for adoption at any time—not
only at birth. You may decide to parent him or her

and find after a few months that it is too difficult.
You can decide to place then. Sometimes things
happen even later that make it too difficult to
parent your child. The steps will be the same no
matter when you decide to place your baby. You
should still go through the counseling (both before and after), seek out an agency or lawyer,
determine the type of adoption you would like,
and once the decision is made, sign the consent
papers.

If you do decide to place your baby, there are
many choices ahead for you and the other birth
parent. This book will present you with options,
teach you the terms used, and help guide you
through the process. But remember that deciding
to place your child for adoption is a very difficult
and emotional decision—no matter when it occurs
in your child's life.

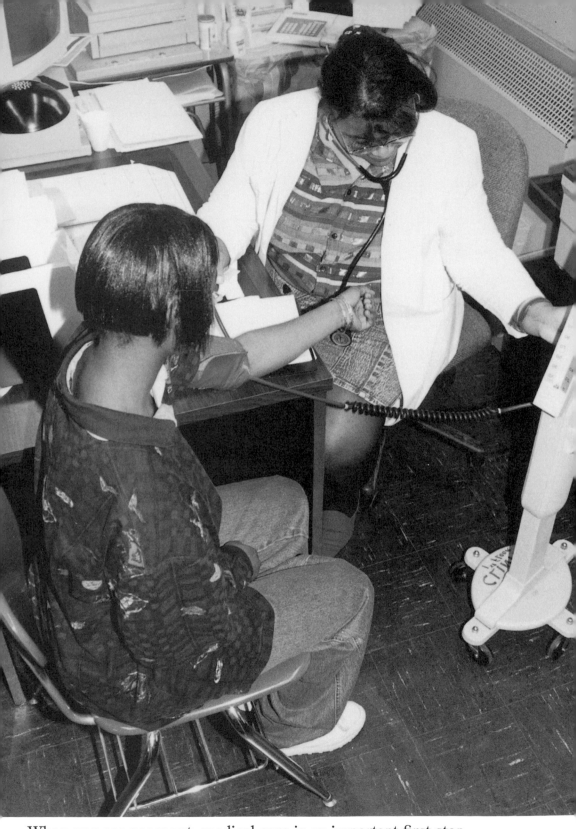

When you are pregnant, medical care is an important first step.

# Chapter 1

# It's up to You

If you find that you are going to have a baby, you may have many new and mixed emotions. These are normal feelings. You and the other birth parent are now faced with an important decision. No one should make this decision for you. With all of the physical and emotional changes that occur during pregnancy, it can be a confusing time for both birth parents. You need to learn about and review all of your options. Take the time to learn about *all* the available choices then make the decision that is best for you, the other birth parent and your baby.

## Medical Care

If you are the birth mother, the first thing you need to do is receive medical care. Prenatal care is very important for all pregnant women. A doctor will advise you on ways to keep your unborn baby healthy. If you do not feel comfortable seeing your family doctor, you can find either low-cost or free women's clinics through the Yellow Pages in your telephone book.  As a father or friend, you can go with the mother to the doctor's office or clinic. She will need support.

## Counseling

When making important decisions, it is best to seek advice from people who can explain your options to you. It will help to find someone who knows about the adoption process and talk to him or her about your feelings.

If possible, talk to your parents, older siblings, or an adult relative. Your family members can be a great source of support for both you and the other birth parent. Even if they are upset when you first tell them that you are having a baby, their feelings can change as you include them in your decision-making.

If you go to a counseling agency for help, make sure that you learn about the full range of services the agency offers. Keep in mind that many agencies also arrange adoptions. If you haven't made up your mind yet, you first may want to speak to someone who is not involved with arranging adoptions in order to receive objective advice.

Counselors can help you decide if adoption is the right choice for you and your baby.

Other people can help you sort out your thoughts and feelings as well as give you important information about adoption. Talk to a doctor, a counselor, or a professional at a women's clinic or pregnancy crisis center. A list of helpful agencies is given in the back of this book. The National Adoption Information Clearinghouse (NAIC) can provide you with a list of pregnancy crisis centers and adoption agencies in your area. You may also find support from a teacher or school counselor, a priest or rabbi, or an adult friend.

No matter where you go for counseling, a good counselor should always treat you with respect and make you feel good about yourself and your decision.

## Making a Choice

The following questions may help you think clearly about adoption and prepare you to talk to your parents about your choices. Be honest with your parents and with yourself. It may be helpful to write your answers down.

- Do both you and the other birth parent want to place your baby for adoption?
- Are either set of parents pressuring you to place your baby for adoption?
- Have you considered abortion?
- Have you thought about marrying the father or mother of your baby and parenting your baby together?
- Have you thought about parenting your baby alone or with the support of your family? Could you live at home? Could you finish school? Could your mother, father, aunt, uncle, grandmother, grandfather, or other relative or family friend help with child care?
- How would you support yourself and your baby? Where would you live?

Placing your baby for adoption is a difficult decision. Adoption is permanent. The adoptive parents—the couple adopting your baby—will raise your child and have legal authority for his or her welfare. You need to think carefully about the questions asked above. Pay attention to your feelings as you and the other birth parent make your decision.

If you decide on adoption, you should find an agency or lawyer that will honor your wishes. You do not have to deal with anyone who tries to make your decision for you. There are a number of organizations in the help list in the back of this book that will assist you in placing your baby.

Remember that adoption is not about giving your baby away. It is a decision made because you and the other birth parent cannot, or do not want to, parent your baby. Adoption is about you making a plan for your baby's life.

If you are thinking about adoption, the more you know and understand, the better you will feel about your decision. Share this book with your family.

No matter whom you turn to for help, always remember that the choice to place your baby for adoption is yours and the other birth parent's to make.

# Chapter 2

# Understanding Adoption

According to the American Academy of Adoption Attorneys (AAOAA), more than one half million people are directly affected by adoption each year in the United States. Adoption is a personal and often very difficult decision. It is the process by which the birth parents decide that they cannot or do not want to be parents to their child. They then place their child and waive their parental rights. If the father is unknown, the birth mother may agree to the adoption alone.

There are many issues and emotions to think about when considering adoption. Your choice will affect you and your baby for the rest of your lives. Therefore this decision should only be made after intensive counseling, and with a thorough understanding of the adoption process.

Once the decision to place your baby for adoption has been made, you and the other birth parent will need to find either an adoption agency or an adoption lawyer to help you through the process. We will discuss the role of each as well as the important things to look for in an agency or lawyer in the following chapter.

The many terms involved in the adoption process can make your decision a confusing and scary one. But if you learn the specialized words and terms, or jargon, you and the other birth parent can make a more informed decision. You will also be able to communicate your concerns and wishes to the agency, lawyer, and adoptive parents.

When people talk about the adoption process you will often hear about the triad of adoption. This refers to the three main groups of people directly involved in all adoptions. They are

- **birth parents** the biological mother and father of the baby;
- **adoptive parents** the couple that adopts the baby;
- **adoptee** the child (and, later, the grown person) who is adopted.

## Consent Papers

If you choose to place your baby, you must sign consent papers after he or she is born. These are legal papers that document your decision to waive the right to parent your child. By signing the

An adoption is made legal when you sign the consent papers.

consent papers, you agree to obey the laws of adoption.

Most states require a waiting period before you are allowed to sign the consent papers. The time varies from state to state. In some states it is as little as forty-eight hours after the birth of your baby and in other states it is as much as ten days. Either the agency or your lawyer should tell you and the other birth parent the time required by your state.

It is important to remember that these papers are permanent. The decision to waive parenting rights is a difficult one. Both birth parents need to think seriously about this decision and make sure that it is the right one.

# Types of Adoption: Open or Closed

There are two different types of adoption that are available to you. Not all agencies will offer you a choice of the two, but it is your legal right to choose either one. Be sure to find an agency that will listen to you, work with you, and give you the help you need to make the adoption plan for your baby that you feel most comfortable with.

Learn all you can about both options. Think carefully about which option sounds best to you, and be sure to talk over the advantages and disadvantages of both before you decide. Your choice will affect your relationship (if any) with the adoptive parents, and your future relationship (if any) with your baby.

**Closed Adoption.** Closed adoption means the adoption is completely confidential. The adoption agency (either public or private) chooses the adoptive parents. Adoptive parents are given background information about both birth parents. They will need this information, such as medical background, to take care of the child. As a birth mother or father, you are not allowed to meet the adoptive parents. You never meet or talk with each other.

When you sign the consent papers, you sign the rights to parent your child over to the agency.

Once the agency finds adoptive parents, the agency will sign the rights over to them.

You are no longer part of the adoption process once you sign the consent papers. Often you may still receive counseling from the agency, but you will not be allowed to participate further in the actual adoption. You will not be told the location or condition of the baby. You will be discouraged from looking for and contacting the adoptive parents of the baby.

If you would like to know something about the adoptive parents or even have contact with them, you may want to consider having an open adoption.

**Open Adoption.** Open adoption means that the birth parents and the adoptive parents share information, directly or indirectly, and possibly meet face-to-face. They could even agree to have some form of contact and communication in the future.

There are many different levels of open adoption. In the most restrictive, the agency or lawyer will show you descriptions and pictures of many adoptive families. You will be allowed to choose the family with whom you would like your child to be placed.

In more open adoptions you might be encouraged to speak with the family on the telephone and exchange first names. In even more open cases you might meet the adoptive family. In what is called "fully open adoption," you and the

An open adoption may allow you to remain a part of your baby's life.

adoptive parents may share your full names, addresses, and telephone numbers. You may stay in contact with the family and your child over the years. It is up to you and the other birth parent to tell the agency or lawyer what you want for you and your baby.

It is important to realize that open adoption is not a type of "co-parenting." The adoptive parents will be completely and solely responsible for the child's safety and happiness.

Without proper counseling, open adoption can be very difficult. A number of very natural but strong emotions can arise on both sides. Before the consent papers are signed, it is best to write up a contract stating the terms of future contact between you, the adoptive parents, and the adoptee. This should be written up with the help of a lawyer so that everything is clear. Recent court cases have found these agreements to be legally binding.

Many adoption agencies and lawyers specialize in open adoption. They are experienced with the common issues that turn up, and the emotions you may be feeling. The NAIC has a list of such people in your area. But be aware that each agency or lawyer defines open adoption differently. Make sure that the agency or lawyer you choose will listen to what you want.

Open adoptions are becoming more and more popular. All major national adoption conferences in the United States are presenting open adoption as the healthiest adoption method for the adoptee. The California Longitudinal Study on Adoption reported that "children of open adoption have fewer behavioral problems than children of closed adoption." Also, most birth parents like the idea of being able to have a say in the placement of their baby. They like knowing something about the family. And, in the best cases, they are happy that they can continue to be a part of their baby's life.

## What Are Adoption Records?

When a baby is born, a document containing his or her birth certificate is created. It lists the names of the biological, or birth, parents. This is called a legal record. In most adoption cases, these records are sealed forever and remain completely confidential. They can only be opened in special cases, such as a medical emergency. You must go to court to have the records unsealed. It is a lengthy and expensive process.

In cases of adoption, a new birth certificate is issued for the baby after the consent papers have been signed. Once the adoption takes place, the adoptive parents are given an amended birth certificate listing *their* names as the baby's parents. A copy of the amended birth certificate is then attached to the original birth certificate and sealed in a vault.

It's okay is to be confused. Adoption is a difficult decision which will affect many people. A good counselor can help you cope with your feelings.

Many adoptees are unhappy with the secrecy. They feel that they have a right to know the identities of their birth parents. Because of this, a few states have created open records. This refers to a legal policy that allows adopted children to see their original records. Currently, Alaska, Kansas, and Tennessee are the only states that allow open records.

Many countries in the world have open adoption records. These include Australia, Canada, Finland, Great Britain, Israel, Japan, the Netherlands, New Zealand, and Scotland.

## No Turning Back

Remember that adoption is permanent. Once the consent papers are signed, the baby is no longer legally yours. This is true for whatever type of adoption you choose for your baby. This is something you need to think about very seriously. You need to make sure that this is the right decision for you and the other birth parent.

In some cases birth parents feel pushed into their decision. After signing the papers, they feel that they have made a mistake. That is why it is so important to find a good counselor or social worker who knows about the adoption process. He or she should talk you through all of your options, as well as the many feelings you may experience before you make your decision. He or she should also be available to talk to you after the adoption. You may feel sad and alone, or you may feel like you made a wrong decision. A good counselor will be able to help you cope with your feelings of loss. If, after counseling, you still feel you made a mistake, you should ask your agency or lawyer about the revocation period for your state.

The revocation period is a determined amount of time (varying from state to state) after the signing of the consent papers in which the birth parents can reclaim parental rights to their baby. In some states there is no such period but in others the time can be as long as six months.

The time to ask questions and explore your options is before you and the other birth parent sign the consent papers. For the benefit of all the people involved, realize the consequences of your decision *before* you sign the consent papers, not after. In cases where the birth parents try to reclaim the baby, it is a very traumatic time for everyone involved—especially for the baby.

# Chapter 3

# Outside Help: Agency or Lawyer?

Once you and the other birth parent decide on the right type of adoption, you need to seek help in finding adoptive parents.

Be aware, however, that adoption laws vary greatly from state to state. This can make the adoption process very confusing. What is illegal in one state may be accepted in another. It is very important to find a good adoption agency or lawyer who knows the laws of your state.

According to the National Council for Adoption (NCFA), of adoptions in 1992, 39 percent were handled by public agencies, 29 percent by private agencies, and 31 percent by private individuals. You and the other birth parent need to look at all of the options and choose the one that best suits your needs.

An agency will help clarify the adoption process for you. If you want, they will also help you select adoptive parents for your baby.

## Public Adoption Agency

These agencies are available in every state. They receive government funding and tend to prefer closed adoptions. However, some will perform open adoptions.

Explain to the social worker the type of placement you and the other birth parent would like for your baby. Ask lots of questions to make sure you understand the rules of the agency. Remember, a good agency will strive to address your needs and concerns. If you do not feel comfortable, call another agency. It is important that you find an agency that will work with you, not against you.

Most agencies should offer counseling before, during, and after the adoption process free of charge. Many will also offer legal services. Be sure to find this out ahead of time.

Both the social services office and the NAIC should have a list of licensed public agencies in your state.

## Private Adoption Agency

There are several types of private adoption agencies. Some specialize in open adoptions, others do not. It is important to determine the practice of the agency before you decide to place your child through it. When you talk to a social worker, ask him or her questions. A few important issues include:

- counseling for both birth parents—even after the consent papers are signed,
- financial assistance with legal and medical expenses,
- information available on adoptive parents.

The social worker may ask you a number of questions regarding you and the other birth parent. He or she may ask about your background, and what you and the other birth parent like to do. With these answers, the social worker can better place your baby with the adoptive parents.

The services available from private agencies vary greatly. Some provide continued schooling,

job training, and housing during the time of your
pregnancy, free of charge. A good way to find one
that best fits you and the other birth parent is to
call many different agencies. Find out what they
offer *before* making your final decision.

Private agencies will often specialize in certain
types of adoption. For example, they may only
place babies of color, or those with special needs.
If you would like to find out about one of these
agencies, many adoption organizations will have a
list of those in your area.

Many private agencies are listed under "adoption agencies" in the Yellow Pages of your local
telephone book. The NAIC should also have a list of
private agencies in your area.

## Private or Independent Adoption

An adoption arranged without an agency is
called an independent, or private, adoption. It is
legal in many, but not all, states. With a private
adoption you directly contact the adoptive parents.
You then seek out an attorney to represent you,
and the adoptive parents do the same. Because you
choose the birth parents and arrange the adoption
with them, this is considered an open adoption.

When you and the other birth parent sign the
consent papers, you will sign the rights to parent
your baby directly over to the adoptive parents.

With a private adoption, you will need to seek
outside counseling. Your lawyer may not offer you

the option to seek counseling. He or she may even try to discourage you from going, but it is very important that you insist. It will help you deal with the emotional issues that you will experience during and after the adoption process. There are many counselors available who specialize in adoption issues. For a list of those in your area, contact the NAIC.

**Legal Aid.** Be sure to look for an attorney that will not charge you a fee if you decide not to place your baby. Legal Aid is a free service available in most places for people who cannot afford a private lawyer.

**Adoptive Parents.** There are many different ways to go about finding adoptive parents for your baby. Some of the more common resources are personal ads, your doctor, or adoptive parent support groups. The Independent Adoption Center in Pleasant Hill, California, works with prospective adoptive parents who want to arrange adoptions directly with birth parents.

It is very important to have a separate lawyer from the adoptive parents. You need a lawyer to help you understand and protect your legal rights as birth parents. Also be very sure that you trust the new family, and that you will be happy placing your baby in their home.

Adoption can be a very wonderful choice if both birth parents agree. With counseling, support, and trust, you and the other birth parent can be comfortable with, and take pride in, your decision.

Adoption is your decision. Do not let other people pressure you into a choice.

# Chapter 4

# Mary and Dave's Story: Making Your Own Choice

The decision to place your baby for adoption is a scary one. It is an emotional time for both birth parents. You may feel vulnerable, alone, confused and maybe even angry. These feelings are normal. But it is very important to make sure that you, as birth parents, understand **all** of your rights, responsibilities, and choices.

In this chapter you will read the true story of two birth parents who placed their baby for adoption. Mary, the birth mother, felt pressured in her decision—pressured by her parents and by the birth father's parents. She felt that other people pushed her into a decision she didn't want. Dave, the birth father, felt left out of the decision. He wanted to help decide what to do about his baby, but no one asked him.

This story will help show you why it is important to learn about all of your choices before you make a decision. If you know your options, and you find people who are willing to discuss all the issues, you and the other birth parent can be sure that the decision you both make is best.

## Mary's Story

*"I was only fourteen and in eighth grade when I found out I was pregnant," says Mary. "My boyfriend, Dave, was sixteen. We both believed that I couldn't get pregnant if it was our first time. We were just too ignorant to use condoms. When I found out I was pregnant, I was terrified. Telling my parents was one of the hardest things I have ever done, but I knew I had to tell them. I was starting to get morning sickness. My mother had said getting pregnant at my age was 'the worst thing that could happen.'*

*"She was crying. I was crying. I threw up and went to my bedroom. That day, I heard my father cry for the first time. When he came to my room, he was so angry that he ripped photographs of Dave off of my bedroom wall.*

*"To make things even worse, Dave's parents didn't want him to be a parent. Because he was in high school and I was in junior high, I wasn't able to see him at school. We were never given the chance to talk with each other about our options.*

*"Because of my religious beliefs, I knew that I wouldn't have an abortion. My parents decided that I would be sent to live with my grandparents during my pregnancy.*

The support of friends and family can help you during this emotional time.

"The day that I was leaving, Dave came over to say good-bye. I was hysterical. He was crying. He didn't know what to do. I was heartbroken and felt ashamed.

"My parents seemed to be making all the decisions for me, and I was afraid to speak up. They arranged for me to speak to a counselor at an agency. Although she was supposed to help me explore all of my choices, she kept talking about adoption.

"She told me about my baby's adoptive parents, how they couldn't have children, how great they were, and how they had already adopted another child. She told me how wonderful it would be for me to give my baby to them and how happy it would make them. She told me that it was the unselfish thing to do, the right thing to do. Then she had me write a list of all the reasons why I wanted my baby to have two parents. Some of the reasons why I thought that adoptive parents would be better were because they would have a car and a house, and they could send the baby to college. I was told that I shouldn't think of parenting my child because I would be a burden to my parents.

"By my ninth month of pregnancy, I was convinced that adoption was the right thing to do. The agency made me feel that I would not be a good parent for my child and that a married couple would be better parents.

"I was in the hospital for less than twenty-four hours, but I did get a chance to hold my baby girl on

*the first day. Once I finally agreed to adoption in the
hospital, I wanted to see my baby one last time. The
hospital advised me against it, saying that I would
get too attached.*

"*I remember being wheeled out of the hospital that
day. I was so ashamed; I couldn't hold my head up.
My mom was crying too. I remember going home,
and I just cried and cried and cried. The next day a
notary and a social worker came over to have me
sign the papers.*

"*Today, I am twenty-nine years old, I am married
to a good man, I have a great job, and in every way
you might think I'm a success. Still, I constantly
think of my baby girl. My 'baby girl' is now a
teenager.*

"*I hope that young people learn as much as they
can about birth control before they decide to have
sex. If a girl gets pregnant, she should know that
there are good people who will help her make one of
the most important decisions of her life. Young people must remember that the decision to parent or
place a baby is theirs to make, no matter what anyone else says.*

"*I'm not against adoption, even after all the mixed
emotions I went through. I'm not saying adoption
isn't right sometimes or isn't right for everyone, but
it should be an educated decision. I had no legal
representation. I had no counseling other than some-
body who was a friend of the adoptive parents and
whose job was to place children because of a belief*

*that it was the right thing to do. I don't think any-
body told me the truth. I was told that my daughter
could always find me if she needed me, and that was
very important. But I was never told that I had to
sign special papers to release identifying information
if I wanted her to be able to find me. I never got the
chance to sign those extra papers.*

*"I believe that no young person should be pres-
sured or forced into placing her baby. I don't think
anyone should try to prevent a young girl or a couple from working together with their families to
make a decision. If I had been encouraged to talk
openly with my parents, maybe I would have had
the chance to talk about raising my baby at home.
It saddens me to say that I was angry with my
parents for a long time after the adoption. Today,
I know that other people got in the way of my
speaking to my own family about a big
decision."*

## Dave's Story

*"I was sixteen when my girlfriend, Mary, and I went
to Planned Parenthood with my older sister,"* Dave
says. *"We suspected that Mary might be pregnant,
and she was given a pregnancy test. When the test
came back positive, Mary and I didn't know what
to do. We didn't know what our options were, or
whom we should tell. We finally realized that we had
to tell our parents.*

*"Mary and her parents stopped by my house to tell my parents about Mary's pregnancy. Her parents were angry with me. My parents didn't handle it well. I felt that the choice for placing our baby for adoption was made by Mary's parents and that my parents agreed with them. I tried to speak up about other options, but neither set of parents would listen to me.*

*"Everyone in our small town knew that I was 'the guy who got Mary pregnant.' Even my friends teased me. I didn't know what to do, so I withdrew from my friends and family. Then Mary was sent to live with relatives out of state.*

*"I felt distanced from Mary and what she was going through. My parents would not allow me to be involved in supporting her during her pregnancy. I didn't know anyone I could talk to. I had never met anybody my age who was a parent. I didn't know any other teenage boy who had gotten his teenage girlfriend pregnant. I felt totally alone.*

*"I look back at my experiences and feel that most of the hard parts of my situation were due to lack of information. I regret that I didn't speak up more strongly about my feelings. I wish there had been an adult who could have given me advice. I also think that there should be a support system within the schools to provide teens with information they might need to deal with difficult situations in their lives.*

*"Most of all, I wish that there had been open communication between everyone involved. Mary and I*

Informing yourself about birth control will help prevent unplanned pregnancies.

*were never allowed to talk about options besides adoption or to discuss how we really felt about placing our baby. I never felt as if I was part of the process of choosing adoption. I just remember that one day I was given consent papers to sign. I never got a chance to see my baby girl.*

*"I would consider adopting a child someday. I don't believe that adoption is wrong. I just think that anyone planning to place a baby and anyone planning to adopt should understand what adoption is all about."*

From these stories we can see that it is important to talk to people who are not directly involved with the adoption. Have them explain all of your choices. Ask lots of questions and talk to them about your own feelings as birth parents. Remember that this is a lifelong decision. Then you can make an informed decision about the choice that is best for you.

# Chapter 5

## Facts for Birth Mothers and Fathers

Here are some important things you should be aware of when you are considering adoption. Knowing the facts can give you the confidence to know that you are making the right decision.

- You have the right to hold your baby before placing him or her with the adoptive parents. You can also name your baby when you sign the original birth certificate.
- After your baby is born you can take as much time as you need to be sure that adoption is the right choice for you. You can sign consent papers in the hospital (if your state allows it) or wait until you are out. Don't let anyone rush your decision. Your baby can go into foster care until you are ready to make your decision. If you then decide not to place your baby, he or she

can be returned to you. Take your time in making your decision.

- Changing your mind *before* you sign the consent papers or *before* the end of the revocation period is within your legal rights. No legal action can be taken against you or your family.
- If you have taken money from adoptive parents or a lawyer during your pregnancy, you may have to return it if you change your mind and decide not to place your baby. However, if you have had adoption expenses covered by an agency, you do not have to pay them back.
- If you place your baby, many support networks are available to help you cope with your feelings of grief and loss. It is important that you talk about your feelings. Don't be afraid or ashamed.
- If you did not have an open adoption, you may be discouraged from searching for the adopted child. Although it is not against the law to search, the ways that you might try to search could be illegal. Be sure to research the laws of your state.
- In an open adoption, written contracts (signed by both the birth parents and the adoptive parents) are usually considered to be legally binding, or recognized by law. Have an attorney check over the contracts. Make sure you and the other birth parent read and understand everything that you both sign. Always get a copy

Adoption laws vary from state to state. Be sure to speak with an agency or lawyer familiar with the laws particular to your state.

of what you sign. It is your legal right as a birth parent to have a copy of all contracts.

- Unless you live in Alaska, Kansas, or Tennessee the adoption records are automatically sealed. With sealed records, the law will not allow any identifying information about you to be released to an adoptee.

- If you do want the adoptee or adoptive parents to be able to find you someday, ask to sign a mutual consent registry. This registry matches the identifying information of adoptees and birth parents. It includes important information, such as current address and telephone number. You must register with this service in the state in which the adoption took place. The registration can take place at any time. You can also give a notarized permission letter stating that you would like to be contacted by either the adoptee or the adoptive parents to the agency or lawyer who handled the adoption. This permission letter can be put in the adoptee's files and will allow the lawyer or agency to release information about you if either is asked by the adoptive parents or the adoptee.

# Chapter 6

# An Adoptive Mother's Story

"*M*y husband and I had wanted children for years," Jane explains. "I could not get pregnant. When we finally decided to adopt, we had the usual closed adoption. We were told very little about the birth parents.

"We ended up adopting two children, first a boy, Evan, and then a girl, Karen. We were open with both children about the fact that they were adopted; it was never a secret in the family. We never thought about the birth parents very much once the adoption was final. We were grateful that we finally had a family, and we considered the children to be our own.

"One day, I received a letter from a woman who said she was Evan's birth mother. I was terrified. I was afraid that the woman would come and take my son away. My husband and I talked for many days before deciding whether to tell Evan about his birth *mother's letter. We decided to be honest and sat Evan down to tell him. Evan seemed to accept the information. 'Is that all?' he said. 'By the looks on your faces, I thought you were going to tell me you were getting a divorce!'*

"*Evan did meet his birth mother and stayed in touch with her through letters and phone calls. He never thought of leaving us for her. We were his parents.*

"*I now run the New Jersey Coalition for Openness in Adoption, a group that tries to change adoption laws so that open records will be the legal form of adoption in New Jersey. I encourage people to set up open adoptions instead of closed ones. I believe that open adoptions are more honest and less traumatic for everyone in the triad. I don't want adoptive parents to live in fear of the birth mothers. I also don't want birth mothers to be shut out of the adoption process. If everyone is open during an adoption process, I believe that a positive, supportive experience can take place.*"

## Adoptive Parents and Their Feelings

The adoption process is an emotional time, not only for you, but for the adoptive parents as well. Adoptive parents are often people who have tried for a long time to have a baby naturally. For some reason, usually medical, the couple cannot conceive a child. The medical process a couple goes

Adoption agencies screen adoptive parents carefully to insure that they will provide a loving and stable home to your baby.

through to try to have a baby can be extremely painful, exhausting, humiliating, and expensive.

When a couple decides to adopt they begin a complicated journey. They must prove to the adoption agency that they are emotionally and financially ready to parent. This is determined through a careful screening process conducted by the agency or lawyer before every adoption application is accepted. State law requires either the agency or lawyer to conduct a home study.

Home study is a screening process for the adoptive parents. They must undergo counseling and interviews and provide personal references. This process helps protect the child and place him or her in the best home possible.

The adoption process can be a very frightening time for the adoptive parents. They have to rely upon the agency or lawyer to help them find a child, and then they have to wait. They may be frightened that one day the birth parents will return and try to take back their child. And worst of all, they must be prepared to accept that the birth mother has the right to change her mind before the revocation period is complete. Upon giving birth, she may decide not to place her child.

You should keep in mind that you are not the only one with mixed emotions during the adoption process. If you choose an open adoption, ideally you and the adoptive parents can support one another through the emotional times.

As a birth parent you can register with a mutual consent registry to aid your child in someday finding you.

# Chapter 7

# An Adoptee's Story

"*I was nine years old when my family told me that I was adopted,*" *Judy began. "My parents, my older brother (who was also adopted), and my older sister (who was not adopted) sat with me at the kitchen table.*

"*My parents had to say it twice because I didn't understand what 'adopted' meant. When I understood what they were saying, I suddenly felt that I was looking at two strangers. Thinking back, I realize that that was silly. They are the only parents I have ever known. I remember running to my room that day, upset and hurt. I gave my parents the 'silent treatment' for three days. After that, I decided that being adopted was not such a big deal. My mother told me not to tell anyone that I was adopted. She was afraid that I would be teased by other children.*

"By the time I was sixteen, I felt that I had nothing to hide and talked openly to my friends about being adopted. It was nice to find out that some of them were also adopted. I began to ask my mother questions about my birth parents. My mother had a paper from the adoption agency with some nonidentifying information about my birth parents: They were both seventeen years old, they both had blond hair and blue eyes (just like me), and my birth father was tall.

"When I called the adoption agency, they gave me a four-page report of more nonidentifying information. I found out that my mother and father had dated throughout high school. My mother was eighteen years old and a freshman in college when she gave birth to me. She had been a local beauty pageant winner in high school. My father was also eighteen, and he had quit high school to take three jobs so he could marry my mother. My father's mother, which would be my natural grandmother, didn't want my father to get married. She persuaded him to move away.

The most interesting thing I discovered was that my birth mother and I have several things in common: We both love kids, the outdoors, and especially swimming. I had been on the swim team for nine years!

"I don't feel bad about being adopted, but I want to know who I am and where I come from. I would like to meet or speak to my birth mother someday.

*My brother, who is also adopted, is not interested in meeting his own birth mother. He is comfortable with the limited information he knows about his birth parents and doesn't feel he needs to know any more than he does. He says he realizes his birth parents placed him with his best interests in mind. That's enough for him."*

## Adoptees and Their Feelings

Some adoptees are initially brought up without knowing they are adopted. They can have many different feelings once they find out the truth. Their feelings are often most significantly affected by how they are told and when they are told.

They may feel angry or betrayed by their adoptive parents for keeping the information from them. They may feel many of the same emotions toward their birth parents for placing them. They may feel confused, alone, and unwanted. But this is usually just an initial reaction. Most adoptees do not doubt that they are loved, and most consider their adoptive parents to be their "real" parents.

Other adoptees are brought up knowing that they are adopted. Even so, they can have mixed feelings about the fact. As they grow older, they may begin to wonder about their biological parents.

## Locating Birth Parents

Sometimes adoptees are curious about their birth parents. As a birth parent it is important for you to think about whether or not you want to someday find, or be found by, your child. This is an important decision that will affect all of you both now and in the future. Think carefully.

In some states, adoptees can request information from the state that can help them find their birth parents. In other states, the records are sealed. Adoptees can also contact the mutual consent registry in the state in which the adoption took place. If the birth parents are also registered, the information may be given to the adoptee. Laws vary from state to state, so it is best to contact the adoption division of your state social services office, or call the NAIC. Most other methods of searching for birth parents can be illegal, so adoptees are not encouraged to search.

An adoptee may find that his or her birth parents asked for confidentiality. In other words, the birth parents did not want to be contacted. Other times the birth parents are eager for contact with their birth children.

Not all adoptees want to find their birth parents, and not all adoptees have negative feelings about their adoption. Everyone has his or her own unique attitudes about adoption.

# Chapter 8

# Your Rights and Feelings

T here are many things to think about if you decide to place your baby. You may feel confused by the terms used in the adoption process. You may feel overwhelmed by the different types of adoption. You may feel that other people are pushing you into a decision you do not want. In Mary and Dave's story, (chapter 4) they each felt as if they had lost control of the adoption process. Having a list of the things you feel are important may help you feel more in control of the situation.

## Your Adoption Checklist

The following list includes some things you may want to request to make sure you have the most open and honest experience when placing your baby for adoption.

55

- If it will make you feel more comfortable, try to select the adoptive parents, especially ones who are willing to have the kind of adoption that you want.
- In an independent adoption, make sure that your own lawyer is present during all adoption arrangements. You should sign your consent papers in front of an impartial third party, someone not involved with the process.
- In a closed adoption, you may want to have a clause in the consent papers stating that you will be notified if the adoption is disrupted or if your baby is not adopted. Babies are not always adopted; sometimes adoptive parents return the baby to the agency or put it into foster care. If this happens with your baby, your life situation may have changed when you are notified. You may want to regain custody of the baby at that time.
- Ask for counseling to deal with the many stages of grief that you may experience once the adoption is final. There are people and support groups that can help you.

## It's Okay to Feel Confused

Once the adoption is final, it is normal to feel sad. You have lost someone in your life, and expressing grief is the way you heal from the loss. You may feel angry. You may feel numb. You may feel denial and disbelief. You may want to be with and raise your baby. You may feel that you made a mistake. These feelings are normal. With proper counseling, you can regain your self-esteem and the pain can become easier to bear.

Any major decision that you make in your life will always affect you. You need to learn how to live with your decisions and feel good about yourself. Some birth parents cope with their grief by writing down their feelings in a letter or poem—even if it is never sent. Others prefer to attend support groups. The NAIC will have a list of support groups in your area.

You may feel that you have abandoned the baby. You should know that you have not abandoned him or her. Instead, you have made a thoughtful plan to provide him or her with a secure, loving home.

As birthmother, it is important to remember that your body goes through many changes both during your pregnancy and after you give birth. Some of your confusion and depression may be caused by postpartum syndrome. This condition, caused by the changing hormone levels in your body, can make you experience very strong mood swings. Your doctor can prescribe medication to help bring your hormone levels under control.

## It's Your Decision

Having information about the adoption process will help make placing your baby much easier. The more you know about the process, the better prepared you will be to ask questions.

Never let yourself be pressured into making a decision that you don't want to make. Take as much time as you need to think about all the options. Ask questions if you do not understand something; as a birth parent you have the right to know. Make sure that you find a counselor or friend to help you deal with the feelings of loss and grief.

Making decisions about your baby is scary. The more you know about all of your options, the easier it will be to make the right decision for you.

# Glossary—*Explaining New Words*

**adoptee**   The person who has been adopted.

**adoption**   The process through which an infant or child is placed in a home with people other than the birth parents. These people are given parental rights of the child. They are responsible for his or her welfare.

**adoption agency**   Public or private organization that arranges an adoption.

**adoption lawyer**   Lawyer specializing in adoption law. In cases of independent adoption, he or she will match the adoptive parents and birth parents, and arrange an adoption.

**adoptive parents**   The couple who adopts an infant or child. They are given legal parental rights and responsibilities for the welfare of the adopted child.

**amended birth certificate**   Birth certificate listing the names of the adoptive parents as the baby's parents in place of the birth mother and birth father.

**birth mother**   Woman who places her biological infant or child for adoption.

**consent papers**   The papers that a birth mother and birth father sign to waive their rights to parent their child.

**home study**   The screening process, required by law, of all adoptive parents before their adoption application can be accepted. It is conducted by the adoption agency or adoption lawyer.

**mutual consent registry**   A database containing information for birth parents and adoptees conducting searches. Participants can register at any time. This is not a legal policy in all states.

**nonidentifying information**   Information, such as interests, hobbies, etc., about the birth parents that can be released to the adoptee if there are open records. The information cannot reveal the identity or location of the birth parents or the adoptive parents.

**open adoption**   Adoption agreement between adoptive parents and the birth parents that allows a set amount of contact with the baby as he or she grows up.

**open records**   Law that allows adoption records to be available to the adoptee, the birth parents, and the adoptive parents.

**revocation period**   The period of time during which the birth parents can change their minds after signing the consent papers. This period varies from state to state.

**triad**   The three groups of people who are part of the adoption process: birth parents, adoptive parents, and adoptee.

# Where to Go for Help

American Adoption
  Congress (AAC)
1000 Connecticut
  Avenue NW
Suite 9
Washington, DC 20036
(202) 483-3399

Birthright
P.O. Box 98363
Atlanta, GA 30359-2063
(800) 550-4900 (hot line)

Independent Adoption
  Center (IAC)
391 Taylor Boulevard
Suite 100
Pleasant Hill, CA 94523
(800) 877-OPEN
Web site: http://
  www.adoptionhelp.org

National Adoption
  Information
  Clearinghouse (NAIC)
P.O. Box 1182
Washington, DC 20013
(888) 251-0075
Web site: http://
  www.calib.com/naic

Nurturing Network
200 Clarktower Place
Suite A200
Carmel, CA 93923
(800) 866-4666 (hot line)

Planned Parenthood
  Federation of America
810 Seventh Avenue
New York, NY 10019
(800) 230-7526

## In Canada

Birthright International
777 Coxwell Avenue
Toronto, ON 34C 3C6
(416) 469-4789

# For Further Reading

Anderson, Carole; Cohen, Mary Anne; and
    Campbell, Lee. *Choices, Chances, Changes: A
    Guide to Making an Informed Choice About
    Your Unplanned Pregnancy.* IA: Concerned
    United Birth Parents, 1989.
Jones, Merry B. *Birthmothers: Women Who Have
    Relinquished Babies for Adoption Tell Their
    Stories.* Chicago: Chicago Review Press, 1993.
Lindsay, J. W. *Open Adoption: A Caring Option.*
    Buena Park, CA: Morning Glory Press, 1987.
————. *Parents, Pregnant Teens, and the Adoption
    Option.* Buena Park, CA: Morning Glory
    Press, 1989.
————. *Pregnant Too Soon: Adoption Is an Option.*
    Buena Park, CA: Morning Glory Press, 1988.
Roles, Patricia. *Saying Goodbye to a Baby: A Book
    About Loss and Grief in Adoption, Volume I.*
    Washington, DC: Child Welfare League of
    America, 1989.
Severson, Randolph W., Ph.D. *Dear Birth Father.*
    Dallas: House of Tomorrow Productions,
    1991.
Sifferman, Kelly Allen. *A Legal Guide for Birth and
    Adoptive Parents.* Hawthorne, NJ: Career
    Press, 1994.

# Index

**About the Author**
Aliza Sherman is a freelance writer based in New York City. She became interested in writing about the adoption process when a friend shared her experiences as a birth mother.

**Photo Credits**
Cover photo by Michael Brandt; photo on page 2 by Guillemina de Ferrari; page 28 by Lauren Piperno. All other photos by Ira Fox.